CD0023S346

THE POWER OF
THEN

THE PATH TO MINDLESSNESS

A Parody by
Dr. Kuda Wooda Shuda, DBs

PETER PAUPER PRESS, INC.
WHITE PLAINS, NEW YORK

To Elton Renfroe—for teaching me
the principles of involved detachment

Designed by Karine Syvertsen

Copyright © 2005
Peter Pauper Press, Inc.
202 Mamaroneck Avenue
White Plains, NY 10601
All rights reserved
ISBN 1-59359-991-9
Printed in China
7 6 5 4 3 2 1

Visit us at www.peterpauper.com

THE POWER OF
THEN

THE PATH TO MINDLESSNESS

A Parody

CONTENTS

INTRODUCTION

The past is not prologue. The past is the future. Or the future is the past. Or the past will soon be the future. Or something. We are writing and rewriting the past and the future, all the time.

The future is coming. It will be here in a moment. Whoops, there it went. You missed it. Sorry. Now that the future has become the past, you can enjoy it in the present. Wrong. You missed the present because you were focused on the past. Nobody's quick enough to apprehend the present because as soon as we perceive it, it's the past.

The past is Then. The future is also Then. There is no Now.

The pages that follow contain what would, to the untrained psyche, appear to be a confusing maze of contradictory language. Not so! Don't read with the mind only. Use your eyes, too. At times I am addressing the being-within-the-being. At times I am addressing my imaginary friend. Sometimes they are the same.

From time to time you may have questions. These are probably irrelevant and will not be answered. The meanings of some words will not be entirely clear to you. Do not despair. Meaning is illusory. Sometimes you will need to understand on the deeper level that is beyond understanding.

When you finish reading this book, you will come away with a deep ennui, and perhaps a feeling of confused contentment. You won't know what the hell is going on, but you will experience the peace of not-caring. In a moment, it will be the past. You will be ready to embrace the Power of Then.

I will be using a simple question and answer format to introduce ideas that will facilitate cyclical reflection and meditation. I call this "The Wheel of Contemplation."

I will also be illustrating many

key concepts with examples. Most of these scenarios fall into the "Coulda," "Woulda," and "Shoulda" paradigm. You will note that these words are also the parts of my name. This is not an accident. It is a function of my highly evolved self-image, or Ego. It is important to enfold your "coulda woulda shouldas" into your model of Then. They are yours. Embrace them.

Dr. K. W. S.

1.

YOU CANNOT "BE" IN YOUR MIND

Our minds are foolish things. They create constructs such as "reality" for which those of us living fully in the Then have no use. Try this simple exercise that will demonstrate the destructive power of the mind and how to avoid it. Pinch the skin of your arm for a few seconds. Hurts, doesn't it? That's the mind at work. Let go. There is no pain. It is past. Pain is in the Then.

You shoulda avoided doing things to cause your false mind to project an image of pain. An image of pain imprisons you in the fortress of your mind. Notice I said "image of pain," not pain itself. We already know that pain is an illusion, because you cannot experience it and perceive your experience of it in the same instant. It is an impossibility. The concept of Now is a terrible master that will enslave you into activities that engage your mind.

When you live in the Then, you are "out of" your mind.

Doesn't "shoulda" require us to act in the Now?

Just the opposite. You cannot perform an action and watch yourself performing that action at the same time. Shoulda is used chiefly in the Was-Then ("shoulda bought Microsoft at $25.00"), but can also be used in the Then-to-Be ("should[a] quit smoking"). You cannot act on shoulda because there is no Now. Nor should you.

What's wrong with reality, anyway?

Here is an example of the unenlightened mind at work. There can be nothing "wrong" with reality because it simply doesn't exist. By the time you get around to thinking about what's happening "now," it is already "then." Then is where all the action is.

The very perception of what is going on around you negates any action. You cannot perceive and act at the same time. Therefore, action is pointless. (It is also exhausting.) You cannot act now because there is no such thing. It is an illusion.

EXERCISE: Try to capture an air molecule with a pair of chopsticks. Repeat. Try it with one chopstick. Try with your hand. Try with two hands. Try with your nose. Give up? Reflect on the idea that all your efforts are already part of your Then experience. There never was any Now.

Trying to grasp the concept of "reality" is like trying to capture the wind with one chopstick.

2.

UNCONSCIOUSNESS: THE WAY OUT OF PAIN

Just because pain is
delivered to your door, you
do not need to sign for it.

Pain—or the illusion that our minds hold onto—is optional. Remember the exercise from the previous chapter? You won't do that again, will you? Had you but known, you woulda avoided such action.

To move beyond pain, you must remove yourself from the energy field of a consciousness clamoring for

Now. There is too much going on there. Let it go. Turn your back on the chaotic voices.

In a vicious cycle, the illusion of Now consciousness creates the illusion of Time. Time is a burden under which we all labor. Most of us can't get enough. What many don't realize is that there is only the Time That Was and the Time That Is To Be. These are aspects of the Then, and they can be controlled. Later. Lay down the burden. Lay it down. Lie down yourself. There, that's better. When you are dreaming, when you have stilled the voices of chaos, you will be fully immersed in the Then. There is no pain.

3.

THE BODY IS AN
AMUSEMENT PARK

Your body can do fun things. Even if you can't stick your elbow in your own ear, you can probably do other cool stuff. You did these things or those things; they are part of your Then experience. They can be again. Again and again in the great Karmic Clothes Dryer (see Chapter 11), you can relive the irreverence of the Then experience. Irreverence can be repeated endlessly. This creates mirth, which we all could use a little more of.

But shouldn't I treat my body as a temple?

Certainly not! You have to be quiet in temples, and not eat in them, and hire all sorts of people to look after them. How can you be healthy if you never say or eat anything, or if you are constantly preoccupied with your appearance? Temples are entirely too much trouble. Amusement parks are much more fun. Try it. If, after trying a course of irreverence and mirth, you decide you want to revert to the temple treatment, it will always be there. It is Then.

Landscaping your
amusement park

The best amusement parks are models of planning and engineering. Your body is no exception. Imagine the landscape of your body at age 21. You were pretty good then, weren't you? Shoulda signed up for that work-out class, right? The Then landscape of your amusement park will be festooned with elaborate topiaries of coulda, woulda, and shoulda.

Planning is crucial. Schedule the

Fun House for Saturday night. Think of Monday morning as the House of Horrors. All the days in between loop along the great roller coaster that is Then. Even if the amusement park is scary at times, we can be comforted by the knowledge that "reality" has no place there.

Don't forget about nutrition in your amusement park. You can eat all the candy you want because you're going to start that diet soon . . . then.

4.

MOVING DEEPLY
INTO THE THEN

THE ZEN OF THEN

A common mistake made by souls embarking on the Way of Then is to assume that the past, being the past, is immutable. Nothing could be further from the truth. As we shape the future, so can we shape the past. Do not be caught up in the fruitless cycle of mindful consciousness. Harness your mental energy to create the Then That Should Have Been. Only then can you move forward into the Then That

Should Be. With practice, the artificial construct "reality" may be totally abandoned. Turn away from the Tao of Now. Your mind is the master— the past and future, its servants.

WHEREVER YOU ARE, BRING A CHANGE OF UNDERWEAR

You might think this woulda been obvious to all. Alas, so many of us wander the earth with our spiritual underwear in tatters. What if a spiritual accident befalls you with your underwear in such condition? What if you are spiritually detained for more than one night? The Zen master Shi-Taos sent two of his students on a long journey. When they returned a year later, one student was careworn, ragged, and in despair. The other one was serene and glowed with an inner light. He described the many adventures that had befallen the pair on their long journey, and how he had come to know peace and tranquility. "I brought extra underwear on my journey," he explained, "and every night I washed out one set in a clear stream. I am clean and refreshed." "What have you learned on your journey?" asked the Zen master. The other student wailed his wretchedness. "I shoulda brought a change of underwear."

5.

THE PATH
OF INERTIA

The path of inertia?
Isn't that a contradiction?

Contradictions can embed us deeply in the web of getting Nothing Done (Chapter 14). Each must be unraveled and followed endlessly, sometimes back to its source, sometimes in a complete circle. Perfect contemplation requires perfect inertia. Be still; and know what Was, and what Could Be— Then. You are not. You could have been, and you still could be. It is for Then to decide.

STRUGGLE IS FUTILE

Struggle is action, and action, even though it is an illusion, removes you from the Then. Ironically, you can imagine struggle, but it is always in the Then. Why cause pain? Who would do such a thing? Do not disturb the perfection of your inertia by fruitless struggle. Struggle can be accomplished later, by others.

THE ART OF FEIGNING INTEREST

Others, who are not attuned to the Power of Then, often clamor for your attention. Many times they will interrupt the flow of inertia by demanding action. Do not act hostile toward such people. It is not their fault; they are as hummingbirds in a grove of blooming rhododendrons. Does the rhododendron feel hostility to the hummingbird? Of course not. The rhododendron remains perfectly,

resplendently still. One might sur-
mise that the rhododendron is even
interested in the frenetic activity
going on all around it. The rhododendron has mastered the art of feigning
interest. The rhododendron cannot be
"interested" in hummingbirds. It is a
plant. Do not forget that. Strive to be
like the plant—fragrant, silent,
immutable.

6.

THE POWER OF SELECTIVE MEMORY: THE PAST IS WHAT YOU MAKE IT

Who owns your Then experiences? Why, you do, of course. You are their creator and master. The past is where your true future lies. You have the power, nay, the responsibility to honor your Then. Make your Then the best it can be, better than it ever was. As a creator, why would you create an inferior being? You wouldn't. You'd craft a splendid being. You are limited only by your own imagination. Give it free rein.

Use all your energy to harness all the Couldas, Wouldas, and Shouldas you can think of. Think of the movie *On the Waterfront* with Marlon Brando. Remember the famous line, "I coulda been a contender"? Brando's character is woefully ignorant of the Power of Then. In your Then, you *were* a contender, and a darn good one, too.

YOUR SPIRITUAL BAGGAGE CLAIM CHECK

Nothing keeps you deeper in the

inertia of Then than spiritual baggage. It is time to retrieve your baggage from the great Cosmic Carousel. When you are weighed down by Couldas, Wouldas, and Shouldas, you can experience the utter serenity of immobility. If your baggage is overweight, so much the better. Sink under its weight. Immerse yourself in the Then. "If only. . ." is a wonderful phrase. Make sure your "if only's" never happen. The irony of "coulda, woulda, shoulda" is that you couldn't, wouldn't, and shouldn't—because it is Then. Reflect on this.

What if I can't find my spiritual baggage?

It is perfectly OK to pick up someone else's baggage, especially if it looks like yours. Other people's baggage may even be more interesting than yours. If you truly can't find your spiritual baggage, you should file a claim with the Astral Travelers' Association, where it will be promptly resolved in about 8,000 lifetimes.

THE SHIFTING SANDS
OF HISTORY

Some history, like the history we read in books, seems fixed and immutable. You say, it happened this way, or that way. But if you think about it, history is being rewritten all the time. Today's conqueror is tomorrow's vanquished.

History is the raw material of Then.

It is said that history is written by the victors. If this is true (and I believe it is), then you are in luck. You are the victor of your own story.

Think of your personal history as the *Rub'al Khali*. The Empty Quarter. Why is it empty? Because you have not written in it. You only think you have. The winds of change can blow over history at any time, rearranging the landscape. Sometimes history takes wild and fantastic forms. If your life has been a whirlwind, slow down and examine each grain of sand. (This should take quite a while and keep you happily occupied in the Then.) Each one is unique and can be arranged in infinite patterns.

When writing your own history, you can employ all the "wouldas" in your arsenal. You woulda cashed in on the Internet boom and got out before the bubble burst, right? You woulda handed that guy his walking papers six months ago, yes? See how easy it is? Your mind holds a cornucopia of information. It is time to put it to use in the Then of History.

7.

UNLEASHING HINDSIGHT: YOUR THIRD EYE IS IN THE BACK OF YOUR HEAD

Writing your own history affords you the unique opportunity to witness and utilize the miracle of hindsight. You have heard about people in cultures in South America and Asia who can access a Third Eye. What you don't realize is that, when you are using the power of Then, your third eye is in the back of your head. Not like your mother had, so that she could see what you were doing when her back was turned, but the Eye of Hindsight.

Hindsight makes everything
crystal clear.

Using your third eye, your Then
unfolds before you in an endless series
of "couldas, wouldas, shouldas." Move
into it. Embrace it. It is not unusual
for people to weep uncontrollably
when they first discover their Eye of
Hindsight. What could you, would
you, should you, have done?

My third eye is having an allergic
reaction. What should I do?

It is common for the third eye to want to ignore the mistakes of the Then, for they could lead to the illusion of pain or discomfort. If you hear your third eye saying "nope, nope, nope, not gonna look, you can't make me look there," you may need glasses to correct your hindsight. Not everyone's born with 20/20 hindsight. You will be amazed at what you coulda, woulda, and shoulda done when you apply the corrective lens of Then.

8.

DON'T BE BOUND BY THE TYRANNY OF THE FACTS

Like history, facts are what you make them. They can be fearsome tyrants. Do not allow them to gain the upper hand. Facts are the handmaidens of Then. Like the master you are, guide your handmaidens firmly, yet gently. They must be compelled to do your bidding (but not anything kinky) at every turn. Think of the facts as a flimsy card table. They can be set up and demolished at will. Upon your table, many a house of cards may be constructed.

And knocked over. This exercise in futility will demonstrate exactly how pointless it all is.

You are the architect. You are the master. Facts are meaningless unless you assign your own specific meaning to them.

But what about immutable facts like gravity?

Gravity is the law. There is no judicial review for gravity. Still, people defy gravity all the time. Their

Then experiences are filled with couldas, wouldas, and shouldas. Coulda used a parachute. Woulda got out of the way of that falling piano if I had seen it in time. Shoulda listened to my mother and not climbed up on the roof. Facts do happen sometimes. It is best to enfold them into your experience of Then and move on. Because so few people use the Power of Then in their daily lives, ideas like gravity become the law. Perhaps one day this will not be so.

When the planet reaches a critical mass of enlightenment, gravity will become just a suggestion.

For further reading, try string theory and quantum mechanics.

9.

BEYOND HAPPINESS AND UNHAPPINESS, THERE IS MORE OF THE SAME

The Sufi mystic Qraq-p'aat once said, "Life isn't one damn thing after another; it's one damn thing over and over."

As a Sufi mystic, he was used to the same thing over and over, because he spent his entire adult life dancing in circles. We can look at Qraq-p'aat's life as a metaphor for the fullness of the Then experience.

Life is cyclical. Life is a dance.

Whether your life is a turkey trot or a tango, you will eventually come around full circle. Happiness and unhappiness are inevitable. They do not happen at the same time. One or the other—sometimes both—happened Then. They will happen again—Then. Do not stop to apprehend them. They are as formless as the mystic dance itself. If you stop, they are already Then. Embrace the timeless rhythm. Trust the dance. There is a certain comfortable consistency in the same damn thing over and over, and sometimes that's the best you can hope for.

10.

ON ADDICTIVE RELATIONSHIPS: THE JOY OF STALKING

So far, we have focused on the interior landscape. How can we apply the principles of Then to our relationships with others? It is easy. Your relationship with the Beloved is an extension of your relationship to yourself. Your interpersonal relationships need never be troubled by concerns of a fictional Now. Instead, focus your energy on the Then to create an idealized image of the relationship that coulda, woulda, shoulda happened.

First, you must erect a giant pedestal. Place the Beloved atop it. Remember the lenses of hindsight we talked about in Chapter 7? It is sometimes necessary to tint these a pleasing shade of pink. The Beloved was perfect. The Beloved had perfect teeth, perfect hair; the Beloved was resplendent in his or her belovedness. But why then is the Beloved not with you? What was wrong with the Beloved that your affection was not reciprocated? It is necessary to return to the Then in order to answer these questions.

Hunt the Beloved down, wherever he or she is. This will afford you the joy of proximity to the Beloved, and allow you to examine each coulda, woulda, or shoulda in its minutest detail. Never is the Then more powerful than when you use it in your personal relationships. You will doubtless arouse strong feelings in the Beloved.

But isn't that counterproductive behavior?

Beloved should have thought of that before he or she moved out, yes? The Power of Then is exactly about counterproductive behavior. There is no other effective way to get Nothing done (see Chapter 14).

RELATIONSHIP ANALYSIS

Review the following questions. A "yes" answer to one or more should signal that you are ready to move into the Then stage of your relationship.

- Does the beloved seem distant, distracted?

- Has the beloved obtained an unlisted telephone number?

- Has the beloved moved to another state?

- Does the beloved call you by

another person's name, especially in the throes of passion?

- Has the beloved entered the Witness Protection Program?

You should also consider the following:

- What has the beloved done for me lately?

- Who does he/she think she is, anyway?

- Who's Chester, and why does he keep calling here?

11.

THE KARMIC
CLOTHES DRYER

Think of the Wheel of Karma as a big clothes dryer. We tumble around and around, touching everything. Everything touches us and moves on. Sometimes we're next to the underwear. (If we read Chapter 4, we would have a spare set.) Sometimes we're tangled up in the silk pajamas. Sometimes we emerge warm and fluffy. Sometimes we shrink. You cannot Be in the Clothes Dryer of Life and apprehend both presence and movement. It is impossible. It can be apprehended only in the Then. You can say, "I was there, Then. I was tumbling with the socks. I moved on." Tumble. Move on. It is past. It is Then. Already you are Elsewhere.

Do not become entrapped in the static cling of Now. So much is tumbling by. If you allow some of it to stick to you, you could receive a nasty shock. Instead, avoid the synthetic experience. Opt for the natural fabric of life. Breathe.

12.

USING AND EMBRACING NEGATIVITY

Isn't negativity bad?

There you go again. If you get caught up in the cycle of thinking negative thoughts about negativity, it will be impossible to break free. It may sound counterintuitive, but open your mind and allow the waves of negativity to break over your consciousness. Happiness is fleeting, but a bad mood can stay with you for days, or a lifetime. A pessimistic outlook will help you to see deeply into the Then.

Couldas, wouldas, and shouldas will be thrown into sharp focus against the dark background of negativity. Negativity can become your greatest tool for moving deeply and passionately into the Then.

Regret is your friend. Cultivate it. A highly developed sense of regret will utterly block you from taking any action in the present. This state of inaction is the culmination of the Power of Then in your daily life.

13.

WHEN DISASTER STRIKES, HEAD FOR HIGHER GROUND

S ometimes the waves of negativity turn into a tsunami. When negativity arises from sources outside our consciousness, it's time to head for the hills. Relationships end. Former lovers seek restraining orders. House-plants die. This is the eternal cycle, and it must be raced away from at breakneck speed. Do not waste any time in the present. Move directly into the Then of regret, or the Then of planning. Facing the facts will only lead to more facts, and who needs those? If you find yourself in a dire situation, it is probably due to an excess of facts.

These events, the faded geranium, the dead budgie—they are already Then! Only by moving away from the present can you fully appreciate Then. You can get a new houseplant—later. Perhaps the former lover will be tormented by an itchy skin disease. All these things are devoutly to be wished for, in the Then that is to be. Imagining your future, or the future of another, can keep you occupied in the Then for decades, thus precluding any action on your part.

14.

HOW TO GET NOTHING DONE

The Greek philosopher Oxymoros once said to his students, "I can't get nothing done because of everything I have to do." One of his students corrected him thus: "Teacher, don't you mean that you can't get anything done?" Oxymoros hit the student with a long stick. "Didn't your mother teach you any manners?" he asked peevishly before returning to his stool to sit immobile for the next 23 years. Nothing was accomplished.

Oxymoros was demonstrating the method of getting Nothing done. We would do well to follow his example.

If you stopped to apprehend every single moment and act on it, you'd never get nothing done. This is not a grammatical error. The Perfect State of Elsewhere, which we will discuss in the next chapter, is a by-product of the splendid inertia of the Then. Paradoxically, this state can be attained only by not-doing. This is the act of doing Nothing. This is surprisingly easy; even a child can do it. If you ask a child, "What are you doing?" he will honestly answer you, "Nothing!" As adults, we have forgotten this state, but we can relearn it.

How can I be "busy" doing Nothing?

Practice saying these mantras to yourself:

- "Tomorrow is another day."

- "I have liberated my mind from the cycle of action."

- "I must consider all my options."

You can move quite comfortably between the Then-That-Was and the Then-That-Is-To-Be, and, through doing so, achieve a perfect state of inaction. You will be getting Nothing done.

15.

THE PERFECT STATE
OF ELSEWHERE

If you faithfully practice all the skills outlined in this book, you will eventually arrive at the utter immobility that many will mistake for serene enlightenment. You will have effectively placed your mind Elsewhere. Elsewhere is a place of your own devising. All your Then wishes, regrets, and fantasies (your couldas, wouldas, and shouldas) can be fully realized, but you will never have to leave the comfort of your own mind.

You will see the present for what

it truly is: an annoying distraction at worst; a pure illusion at best. You are not here. Never having left, you have finally arrived.

Hello, you must be going.